# Beginning Fiddle Duets

## for two cellos

Book One

written and arranged by Myanna Harvey

CHP305

www.charveypublications.com - print books
www.learnstrings.com - PDF downloadable books
www.harveystringarrangements.com - chamber music

# Beginning Fiddle Duets for Two Cellos

Written and arranged by Myanna Harvey

## Table of Contents

# Beginning Fiddle Duets for Two Cellos

## Cripple Creek

Trad., arr. Myanna Harvey

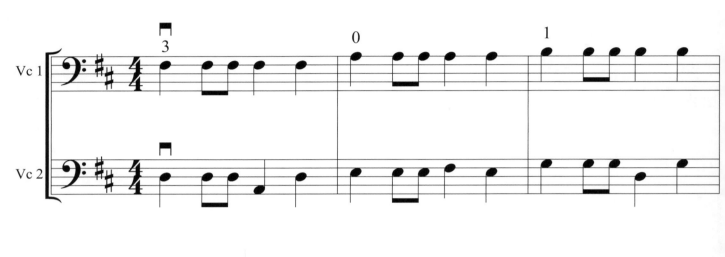

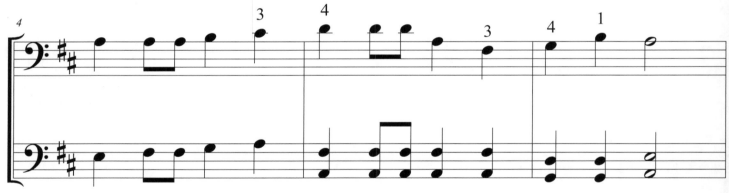

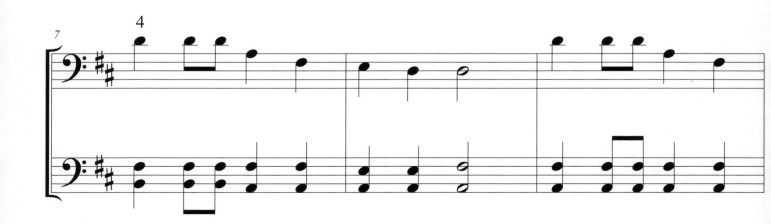

4

# Bingo

Trad., arr. Myanna Harvey

# Drill Ye Tarriers

Trad., arr. Myanna Harvey

# Old Joe Clark

Trad., arr. Myanna Harvey

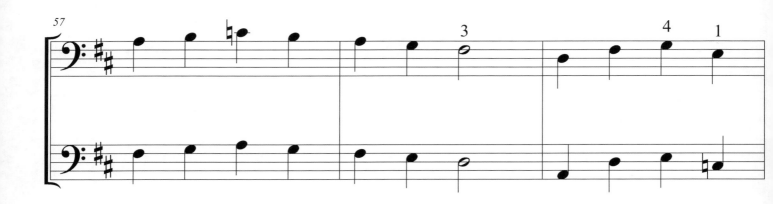

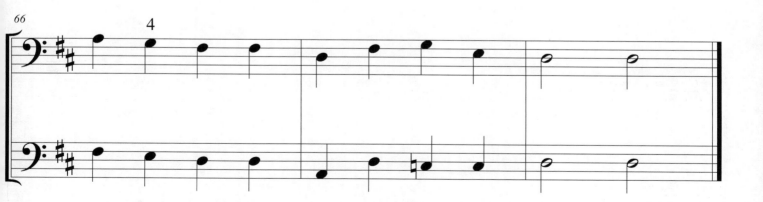

# Erie Canal

Trad., arr. Myanna Harvey

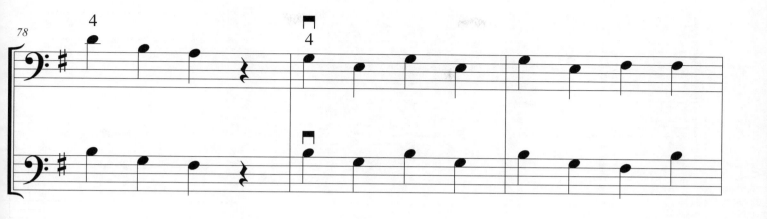

# Arkansas Traveler

Trad., arr. Myanna Harvey

# I Ride an Old Paint

Trad., arr. Myanna Harvey

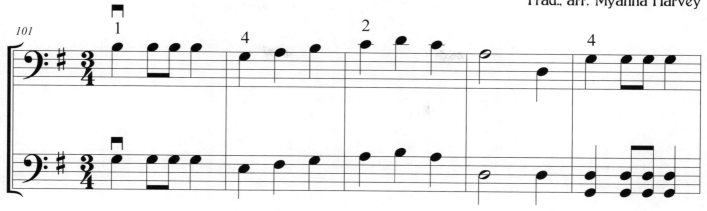

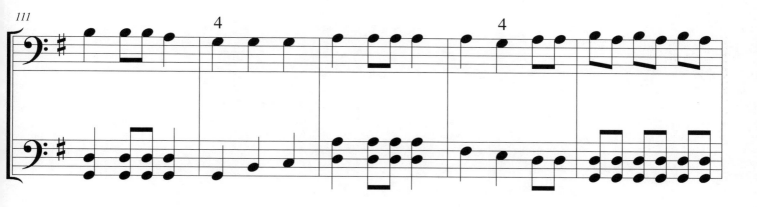

# Battle Cry of Freedom

Trad., arr. Myanna Harvey

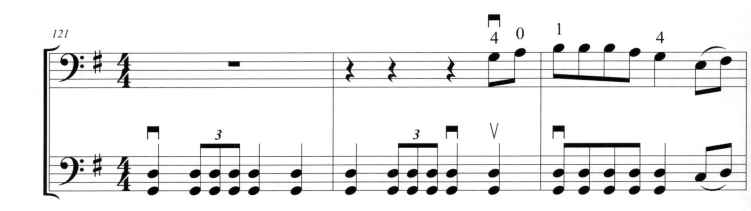

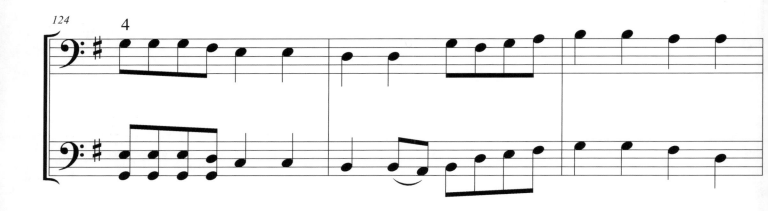

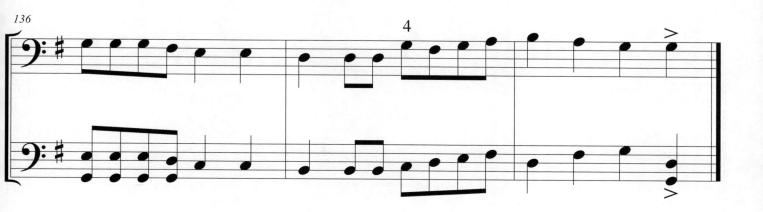

# Goober Peas

Trad., arr. Myanna Harvey

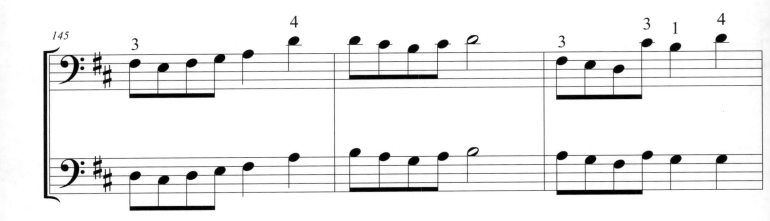

# Aiken Drum

Trad., arr. Myanna Harvey

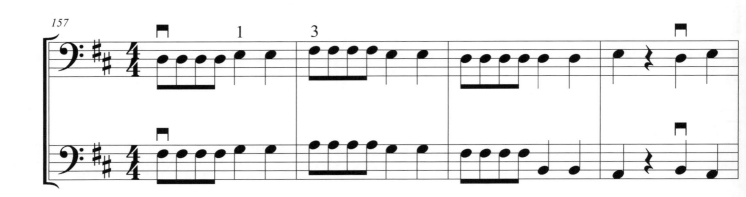

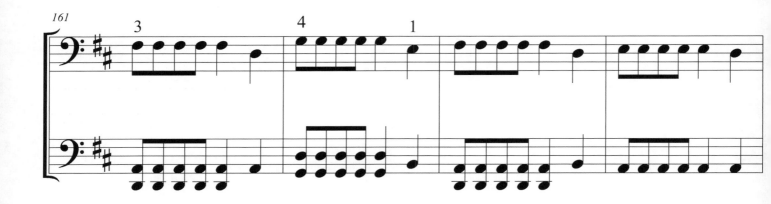

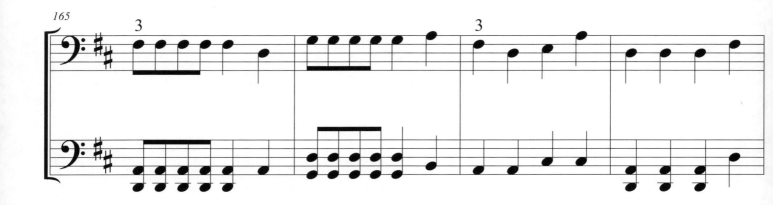

18

# Sailor's Jig

Myanna Harvey

# The Muffin Man

Trad., arr. Myanna Harvey

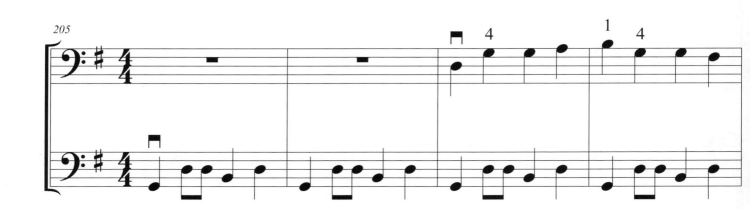

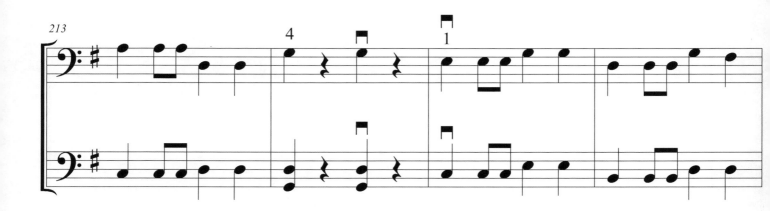

22

# Oh Susannah

Foster, arr. Myanna Harvey

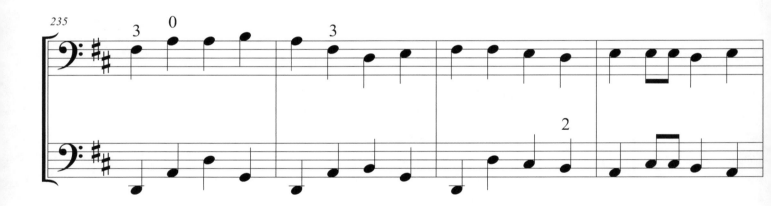

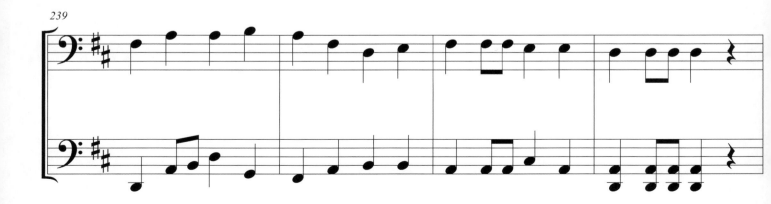

# Yankee Doodle

Trad., arr. Myanna Harvey

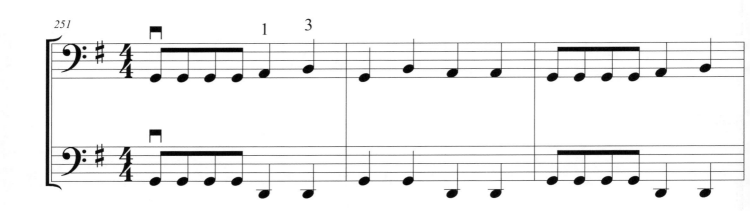

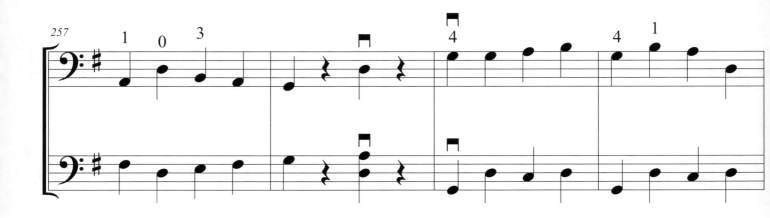

# The Horse and the Flea

Trad., arr. Myanna Harvey

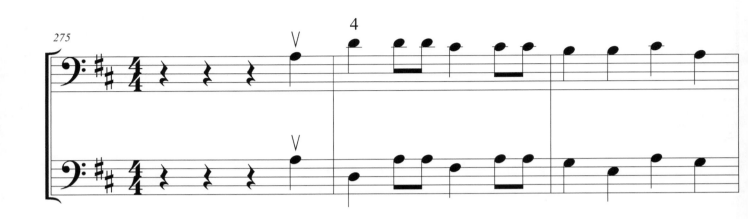

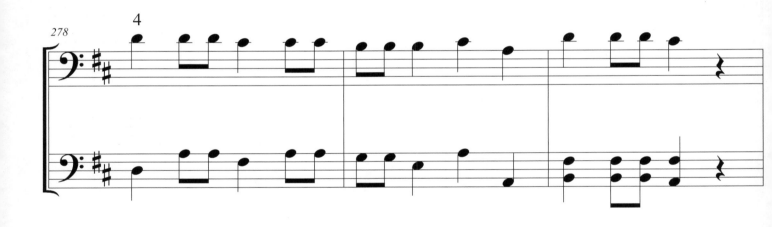

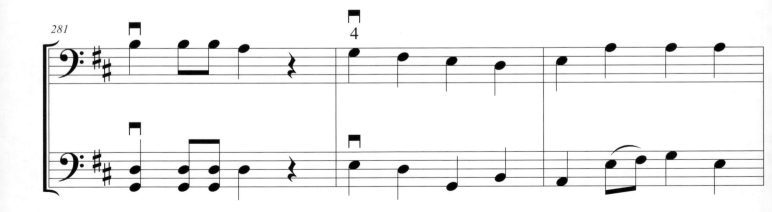

# Piper's Jig

Myanna Harvey

# Camptown Races

Foster., arr. Myanna Harvey

# Kentucky Lullaby

Trad., arr. Myanna Harvey

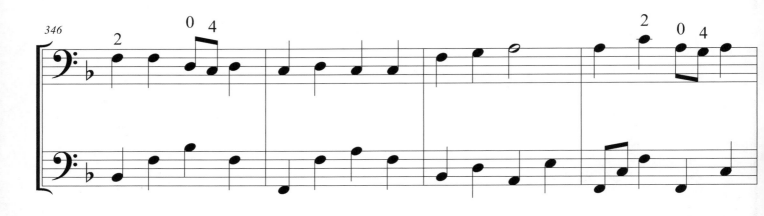

# Flying Fiddle Duets for Two Cellos, Book One

## John Ryan's Polka

Trad., arr. Myanna Harvey

Made in United States
Troutdale, OR
02/16/2024

17713425R00022